Place Value

Grade 2

Frank Schaffer Publications®

Development: MATHQueue, Inc.

Frank Schaffer Publications®

Printed in the United States of America. All rights reserved. Limited Reproduction Permission: Permission to duplicate these materials is limited to the person for whom they are purchased. Reproduction for an entire school or school district is unlawful and strictly prohibited. Frank Schaffer Publications is an imprint of School Specialty Publishing. Copyright © 2005 School Specialty Publishing.

Send all inquiries to:
Frank Schaffer Publications
3195 Wilson Drive NW
Grand Rapids, Michigan 49534

Place Value—Grade 2

ISBN: 0-7682-3112-4

2 3 4 5 6 7 8 9 10 PAT 10 09 08 07 06 05

Table of Contents

Published by Frank Schaffer Publications. Copyright Protected.

Introduction

At the foundation of basic math skills is the place value system. It is important for a child to be able to identify the place value of a number and recognize a number when it is presented in many different forms.

The activities in this workbook provide practice for the following skills associated with the place value system.

- ✔ counting
- ✔ skip counting by 10
- ✔ expanded form
- ✔ estimating
- ✔ rounding
- ✔ number lines

- ✔ standard form
- ✔ word form
- ✔ place value blocks
- ✔ base ten money
- ✔ ordering numbers
- ✔ patterns

Encourage students to be active learners and to use manipulatives whenever practical. It is critical that all students be fluent in modeling numbers using place value blocks. Students need to know and understand why each of the models below represent the same number.

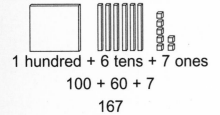
1 hundred + 6 tens + 7 ones
100 + 60 + 7
167

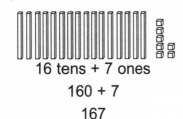
16 tens + 7 ones
160 + 7
167

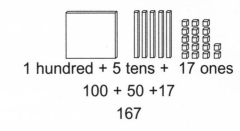
1 hundred + 5 tens + 17 ones
100 + 50 +17
167

Once a child can model, rename, and explain the value related to a number, that child will be able to make the connection on how to transfer what has been learned in doing one problem to the next. At that moment, a child has captured the essence of the place value system.

The activity sheets in the workbook were developed in accordance with standards as prescribed by the National Council of Teachers of Mathematics. Throughout the workbook, concepts are covered by way of the five process strands for mathematics.

Look in the upper left corner of each page to see which process strand is covered on that page. Or check the Correlation to Standards chart on page 6 for a listing of page numbers by process strand.

Published by Frank Schaffer Publications. Copyright Protected.

0-7682-3112-4 *Place Value*

In the early grades building mathematical knowledge through **problem solving** should involve situations that arise in the classroom. Students should solve problems using familiar objects and situations.

Reasoning and proof are fundamental aspects of mathematics that require young learners to make assumptions and to investigate whether their ideas are sound. Encourage students to explain how they solved problems and how they know their answers are correct.

Language is as important to learning mathematics as it is when learning to read. In order to make assumptions and test ideas, students must be able to clearly **communicate** their thoughts. In the classroom provide opportunities for students to meet in pairs or small groups to discuss the methods they used to solve the problems. Encourage students to demonstrate a variety of methods for solving story problems.

It is important that children hear the language of mathematics in meaningful context. To optimize mathematical thinking, create and structure a mathematically rich environment for your students. Exploring their ideas will give your students practice in thinking coherently and communicating ideas clearly to peers, teachers, and others. Model appropriate conventional vocabulary.

When students learn to make assumptions, test their assumptions, and can discuss them coherently, they will be able to recognize and use **connections** among mathematical ideas and to the world around them.

As students begin to recognize multiple **representations** of numbers, they will be able to organize, record, look for patterns, and communicate mathematical ideas. This will enable them to solve problems in multiple ways. As they become comfortable solving problems, they will be able to solve more complicated problems and make predictions. Even very young children can be taught to use models to understand physical, social, and mathematical phenomena.

When students are taught to problem solve, use reasoning skills, communicate mathematical ideas, make connections, and use representation to interpret mathematical phenomena, math will become more than simply numbers and operations. Mathematics will become the key to understanding their universe and how everything in it relates to everything else.

Published by Frank Schaffer Publications. Copyright Protected.

0-7682-3112-4 *Place Value*

Correlation to NCTM Standards

Communication	Connections	Problem Solving	Reasoning and Proof	Representation
14, 15, 17, 21, 39, 44, 54, 55, 57, 61, 73, 75, 83	9, 13, 23, 31, 35, 37, 43, 46 47, 48 51, 63, 77, 80, 82	16, 27, 33, 42, 49, 60, 66, 76, 78, 84	24, 25, 26, 28, 32, 34, 58, 59, 64, 65, 68, 71, 72, 81	10, 11, 12, 18, 19, 20, 22, 29, 30, 36, 38, 40, 41, 45, 50, 52, 53, 56, 62, 67, 69, 70, 74, 79

Published by Frank Schaffer Publications. Copyright Protected.

0-7682-3112-4 *Place Value*

Name_____ Date _____

Pretest

1. Which number has a 3 in the tens place?

   a. 3   **b.** 23   **c.** 132   **d.** 309   _____

2. Bill is thinking of a number that is greater than 11 and less than 19. The number has a 5 in the ones place. What number is Bill thinking of?   _____

3. What is the value of the underlined digit?

   5̲27   _____

4. Write the number 832 in expanded form.

   _____

5. _____ tens and 8 ones is an expanded form of 28.

6. Write 92 in word form.

   _____

7. Write the number that is 10 less than 829.   _____

Published by Frank Schaffer Publications. Copyright Protected.

0-7682-3112-4 *Place Value*

Pretest (cont.)

8. Susie has 53 cents. Susie has _____ dimes and _____ pennies.

9. Count to find the total number of tally marks.

_____

10. Complete the chart for the number 34.

tens	ones

11. Draw place value blocks to model the number 235.

hundreds	tens	ones

12. Rewrite 2 tens and 13 ones in standard form. _____

Published by Frank Schaffer Publications. Copyright Protected.

0-7682-3112-4 *Place Value*

Happy Birthday to Ones

Connections

Draw candles on each birthday cake to match the
number shown on the top of the cake.

1.

2.

3.

4.

5.

6.

Published by Frank Schaffer Publications. Copyright Protected.

0-7682-3112-4 *Place Value*

Name_____ Date _____

Plenty of Fruit

Count how many fruit are in each group.

1.

How many apples? _____

2.

How many bananas? _____

3.

How many bunches of grapes? _____

4.

How many peaches? _____

5.

How many watermelon wedges? _____

Published by Frank Schaffer Publications. Copyright Protected.

0-7682-3112-4 *Place Value*

Groups of 10 and More

Circle a group of 10 in each set.
Fill in the blanks to complete the number sentence.

1.

___10___ + ___6___ = ___16___

2.

_____ + _____ = _____

3.

_____ + _____ = _____

4.

_____ + _____ = _____

5.

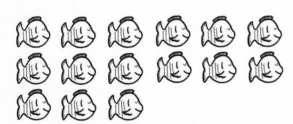

_____ + _____ = _____

Published by Frank Schaffer Publications. Copyright Protected.

0-7682-3112-4 *Place Value*

Match the Carrots

Representation

Match each rabbit with the carrot that shows the number written in word form. Draw a line to show the match.

1.
eleven

2.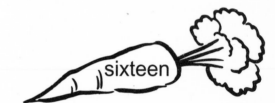
sixteen

3.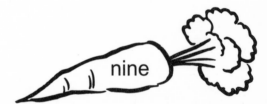
nine

4.
twenty

Published by Frank Schaffer Publications. Copyright Protected.   0-7682-3112-4 *Place Value*

House Numbers

Each house has an address. Color the houses that have an address with a 6 in the ones place.

1.

2.

3.

4.

5.

6.

Published by Frank Schaffer Publications. Copyright Protected.

0-7682-3112-4 *Place Value*

Name_____ Date _____

Pictures and Words

Count how many. Write your answer as a number.
Then write your answer in word form.

1.

_____

_____

2.

_____

_____

3.

_____

_____

4.

_____

_____

Published by Frank Schaffer Publications. Copyright Protected.

Communication

What's in the Picture?

Count the items named in the picture. Fill in the blanks.

1.

There are ____ pancakes.

2.

There are ____ doughnuts.

3.

There are ____ presents.

4.

There are ____ hot air balloons.

Circle the word that best completes each sentence.

5. There are | *more   less* | pancakes than doughnuts.

6. There are the same number of hot air balloons
as | *doughnuts   pancakes* | .

Published by Frank Schaffer Publications. Copyright Protected.

0-7682-3112-4 *Place Value*

Problem Solving

What is Tony's Number?

Tony is playing a guessing game with five friends.
Can you help decide what number Tony is thinking of?

I will give you each one clue.

The number has two digits.

The number is greater than 12.

The number is not odd.

The number is less than 20.

The number has 6 ones.

What number is Tony thinking of? _____

Published by Frank Schaffer Publications. Copyright Protected.

0-7682-3112-4 *Place Value*

Communication

Ones, Tens, Hundreds

275

hundreds place _____↑ ↑ ↑_____ ones place

tens place

Name the place of the underlined digit.

1. 4<u>9</u>6 _____

2. <u>1</u>37 _____

3. 52<u>8</u> _____

4. 3<u>1</u>2 _____

5. <u>4</u>07 _____

6. 6<u>4</u>2 _____

7. 32<u>0</u> _____

8. 92<u>6</u> _____

Give the number in the place named.

9. 256, tens _____

10. 17, ones _____

11. 158, hundreds _____

12. 924, tens _____

13. 340, ones _____

14. 510, hundreds _____

Published by Frank Schaffer Publications. Copyright Protected.

0-7682-3112-4 *Place Value*

Name_____ Date _____

Name That Value

Write the place of the digit that is underlined.
Give its value.

1. <u>2</u>76

_____

_____

2. 61<u>4</u>

_____

_____

3. 3<u>0</u>9

_____

_____

4. 58<u>1</u>

_____

_____

5. <u>5</u>2

_____

_____

6. 1<u>1</u>1

_____

_____

7. <u>7</u>01

_____

_____

8. 8<u>9</u>

_____

_____

Published by Frank Schaffer Publications. Copyright Protected.

0-7682-3112-4 *Place Value*

Name_____ Date _____

Name That Number

Write the number in the tens place.

1. 175 _____   **2.** 521 _____

3. 814 _____   **4.** 98 _____

5. 410 _____   **6.** 160 _____

Write the number in the hundreds place.

7. 285 _____   **8.** 450 _____

9. 962 _____   **10.** 658 _____

Write the number in the ones place.

11. 65 _____   **12.** 19 _____

13. 40 _____   **14.** 64 _____

15. 208 _____   **16.** 370 _____

Published by Frank Schaffer Publications. Copyright Protected.   0-7682-3112-4 *Place Value*

Representation

Name_____ Date _____

How Many?

How many hundreds are in each number?

1. 812 _____ **2.** 514 _____

3. 468 _____ **4.** 230 _____

5. 961 _____ **6.** 657 _____

How many ones are in each number?

7. 25 _____ **8.** 50 _____

9. 92 _____ **10.** 67 _____

How many tens are in each number?

11. 316 _____ **12.** 149 _____

13. 432 _____ **14.** 764 _____

15. 815 _____ **16.** 935 _____

Published by Frank Schaffer Publications. Copyright Protected.

0-7682-3112-4 *Place Value*

Communication

Name_____ Date _____

Value of a Digit

Write the value of the underlined digit in each number.

1.

_____

2.

_____

3.

_____

4.

_____

5.

_____

6.

_____

Published by Frank Schaffer Publications. Copyright Protected.

0-7682-3112-4 *Place Value*

Name_____ Date _____

Rewrite From Expanded Form

Write each number in standard form.

1. 100 + 20 + 8 _____

2. 300 + 60 +2 _____

3. 500 + 90 + 4 _____

4. 100 + 90 _____

5. 40 + 2 _____

6. 700 + 6 _____

7. 800 + 10 + 5 _____

8. 200 + 20 + 2 _____

9. 300 + 90 + 2 _____

10. 400 + 70 _____

Published by Frank Schaffer Publications. Copyright Protected.

0-7682-3112-4 *Place Value*

Don't Look Down

Write the height of the tallest roller coasters in expanded form.

1. Superman: The Escape in California is 415 feet tall.

   _____

2. Tower of Terror in Australia is 380 feet tall.

   _____

3. Steel Dragon 2000 in Japan is 318 feet tall.

   _____

4. Fujiyama in Japan is 259 feet tall.

   _____

5. Millennium Force in Ohio is 310 feet tall.

   _____

Published by Frank Schaffer Publications. Copyright Protected.

0-7682-3112-4 *Place Value*

Name_____ Date _____

Numbers in Standard Form

Write each number in standard form.

1. 2 tens and 7 ones   _____

2. 8 hundreds and 4 tens   _____

3. 1 hundred, 1 ten, and 1 one   _____

4. 8 tens and 0 ones   _____

5. 3 tens and 2 ones   _____

6. 6 hundreds, 5 tens, and 9 ones   _____

7. 3 tens and 1 one   _____

8. 9 tens and 9 ones   _____

9. 1 hundred and 6 ones   _____

Published by Frank Schaffer Publications. Copyright Protected.

0-7682-3112-4 *Place Value*

Reasoning and Proof

What Color is the Wibble?

Color the Wibbles green that make up the expanded form of 832.

Color the Wibbles red that make up the expanded form of 159.

Color the Wibbles blue that make up the expanded form of 673.

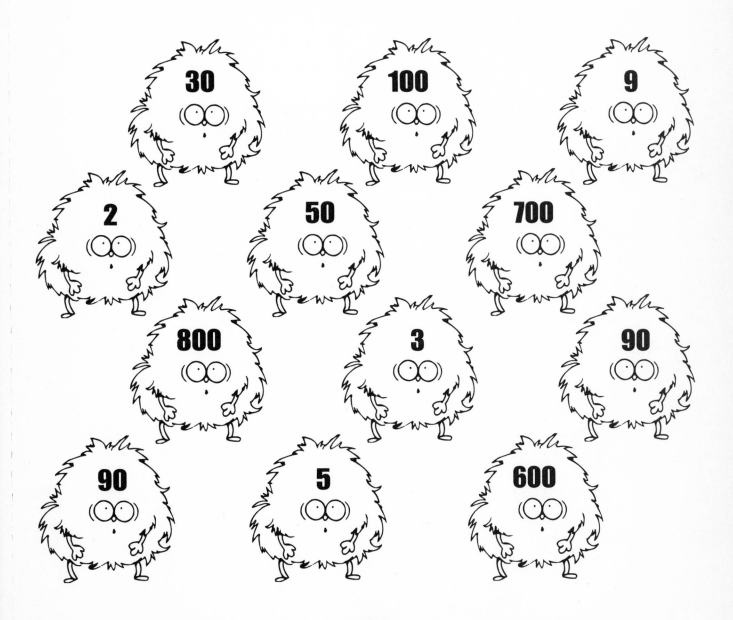

Published by Frank Schaffer Publications. Copyright Protected.

0-7682-3112-4 *Place Value*

Reasoning and Proof

Bunches of Balloons

152	285	335	45	550	506
145	825	305	415	500	652

Write numbers that have 5 in the **ones** place in these balloons.

Write numbers that have 5 in the **tens** place in these balloons.

Published by Frank Schaffer Publications. Copyright Protected.

0-7682-3112-4 *Place Value*

What Number Am I?

Name each number described.

1. The digit in the tens place is the same as the digit in the ones place. The digit in the ones place is 4.   _____ _____

2. The digit in the ones place is odd and less than the digit in the tens place. The digit in the tens place is 2.   _____ _____

3. The digit in the ones place is one more than the digit in the tens place. The digit in the tens place is 5.   _____ _____

4. The digit in the tens place is 1 greater than the digit in the ones place. The digit in the ones place is 8.   _____ _____

5. The digit in the tens place is half of the digit in the ones place. The digit in the ones place is 6.   _____ _____

6. The digit in the ones place is one greater than 5. The digit in the tens place is one greater than 6.   _____ _____

Published by Frank Schaffer Publications. Copyright Protected.   0-7682-3112-4 *Place Value*

Who is Reading What Book?

Reasoning and Proof

Each child reads one of the books below. Match each child to the book described.

1.
Sally

I am on a page with an even number in the ones place.

2.
Marc

My book has at least one hundred pages.

3.
Joel

I am reading a book that had the same digit in ones, tens, and hundreds places.

4.
Myra

I finished my book already. There were less than thirty pages to read.

Published by Frank Schaffer Publications. Copyright Protected.

0-7682-3112-4 *Place Value*

Color to Reveal

Look at the number in each section. If the digit in the tens place is greater than 3, but less than 8, color that section red. Color all other sections blue.

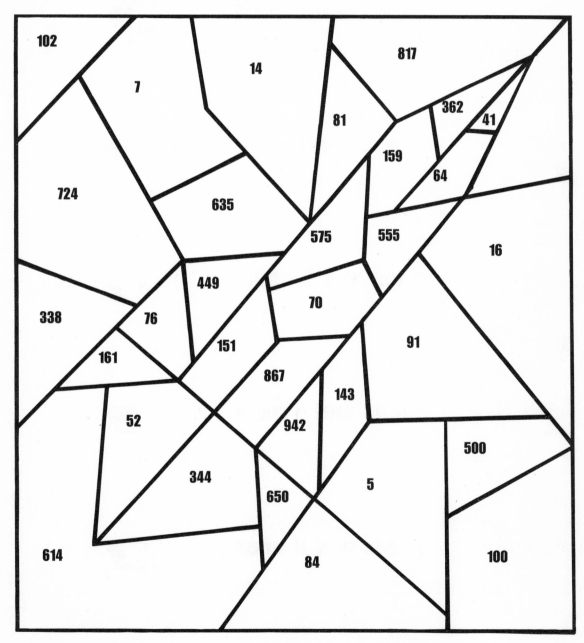

Published by Frank Schaffer Publications. Copyright Protected.

0-7682-3112-4 *Place Value*

Banners of Numbers

Write each number in standard form.

1.

 **4 tens and 8 ones**

48

2.

 **6 tens and 1 one**

_____

3.

 **1 ten and 5 ones**

_____

4.

 9 tens and 4 ones

_____

5.

 **8 tens and 8 ones**

_____

Published by Frank Schaffer Publications. Copyright Protected.

0-7682-3112-4 *Place Value*

Who Lives Longer?

Use the table of life spans to answer each question.

Do You Know? Science

1. Which animal has a life span that has 1 ten and 8 ones?

_____

2. Which animal lives half as long as the Bald Eagle?

_____

3. Which animal's life span is 20 tens?

_____

4. Which animal's life span is 70 + 2?

_____

5. Which animal's life span is 4 tens?

_____

Animal	Average Life Span in Years
Tortoise	200
Box turtle	100
Blue Whale	80
Human	72
Alligator	50
Bald Eagle	40
Dolphin	30
Horse	20
Black Bear	18
Tiger	16
Cow	15
Sea Lion	12
Goat	8
Kangaroo	7
Mouse	3

Published by Frank Schaffer Publications. Copyright Protected.

0-7682-3112-4 *Place Value*

Reasoning and Proof

Name_____ Date _____

What is Missing?

Fill in the blanks to make a true statement.

1. Five hundred forty-three is written as _____.

2. _____ tens and 6 ones is the expanded form of 86.

3. 385 means 300 + ____ + 5.

4. 2 tens and 2 ones are the same as _____ + 2.

5. One hundred _____ is written as 111.

6. Nine hundred forty-four means 900 + _____ + 4.

7. 215 written in words is two hundred _____.

8. 700 + 50 + 7 is the expanded form of _____.

Published by Frank Schaffer Publications. Copyright Protected.

0-7682-3112-4 *Place Value*

Name_____ Date _____

Find Each Path

Find the path that leads to the standard form of each number at the bottom of the puzzle. Begin in each square at the top of the puzzle.

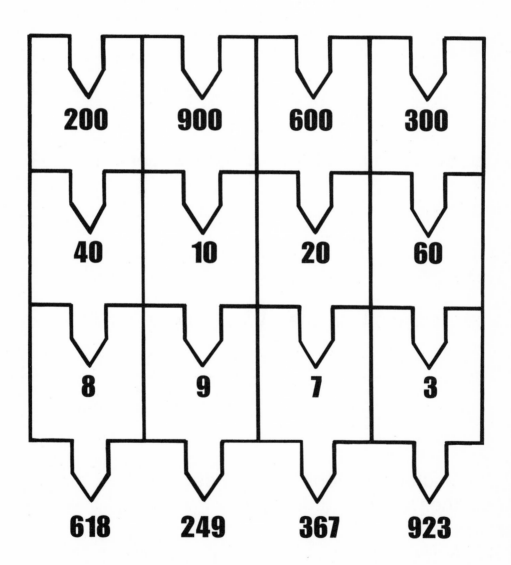

Published by Frank Schaffer Publications. Copyright Protected.

0-7682-3112-4 *Place Value*

Reasoning and Proof

Name_____ Date _____

Place Value Riddles

Read the riddle. Circle the answer.
Then write a riddle for the other number.

1. I have 7 tens and 9 ones. What number am I? | 79   97 |

New riddle: _____

_____ Answer: _____

2. I have an even number of tens. What number am I? | 54   83 |

New riddle: _____

_____ Answer: _____

3. I have one less ten than ones. What number am I? | 12   32 |

New riddle: _____

_____ Answer: _____

4. I have 8 hundreds, no tens and 2 ones.
What number am I? | 802 820 |

New riddle: _____

_____ Answer: _____

34

Published by Frank Schaffer Publications. Copyright Protected.

0-7682-3112-4 *Place Value*

Name_____ Date _____

Building Ice Cream Cones

In each ice cream cone below, a number is given in standard form. Use numbers in the box to make the expanded form of the number.

Write the number of hundreds in the top scoop.

Write the number of tens in the middle scoop.

Write the number of ones in the bottom scoop.

40	900	2	80
200	9	300	70
1	700	8	50

281 749 352 978

Published by Frank Schaffer Publications. Copyright Protected.

0-7682-3112-4 *Place Value*

Representation

Name_____ Date _____

Expanding a Number

Fill in the blank to write each number in expanded form.

1. 78   _____ + _____

            _____ tens _____ ones

2. 25   _____ + _____

            _____ tens _____ ones

3. 14   _____ + _____

            _____ ten _____ ones

4. 41   _____ + _____

            _____ tens _____ one

5. 92   _____ + _____

            _____ tens _____ ones

6. 50   _____ + _____

            _____ tens _____ ones

Published by Frank Schaffer Publications. Copyright Protected.   0-7682-3112-4 *Place Value*

Connections

Name_____ Date _____

Take the Elevator

Match each building's height with its expanded form.
Write the letter of the expanded form in the blank.

Do You Know? Social Studies

1. Sears Tower in Illinois is 1,450 feet tall. _____

2. Citic Plaza in China is 1,283 feet tall. _____

3. Petronas Towers in Malaysia is 1,483 feet tall. _____

4. Jin Mao Building in China is 1,381 feet tall. _____

a. 1,000 + 200 + 80 + 3   **b.** 1,000 + 400 + 50

c. 1,000 + 400 + 80 + 3   **d.** 1,000 + 300 + 80 + 1

Published by Frank Schaffer Publications. Copyright Protected.

0-7682-3112-4 *Place Value*

Name_____ Date _____

Picking from the Apple Tree

Write the number that is inside each apple in expanded form.

1. **123**

_____

2.  **52**

_____

3. **813**

_____

4. **706**

_____

Write the standard form of each number.

5. 800 + 30 + 2 _____

6. 200 + 40 _____

7. 100 + 6 _____

8. 500 + 50 + 1 _____

Published by Frank Schaffer Publications. Copyright Protected.

0-7682-3112-4 *Place Value*

Communication

Write the Number

Write each number that is described.

1. I have 8 hundreds, 7 tens, and 3 ones. What number am I?

   _____

2. I have 300, and I have a 2 in the tens place. I also have a 4 in the ones place. What number am I?

   _____

3. I am greater than 500 but less than 700. I have no tens and no ones. What number am I?

   _____

4. I have 6 ones. The digit in my tens place is one more than the digit in my ones place. What number am I?

   _____

5. I have 6 hundreds. I have 2 tens less than 6 tens. I have 1 one. What number am I?

   _____

6. I have an odd number of ones. My ones digit is greater than 3, but less than 7. I have the same number of hundreds, tens, and ones. What number am I?

   _____

Published by Frank Schaffer Publications. Copyright Protected.

0-7682-3112-4 *Place Value*

Name_____ Date _____

Ten More or Ten Less

Write the number that is 10 more than the number given.

1. 18 _____

2. 85 _____

3. 13 _____

4. 67 _____

5. 42 _____

6. 22 _____

7. 51 _____

8. 39 _____

9. 70 _____

10. 112 _____

Write the number that is 10 less than the number given.

11. 163 _____

12. 140 _____

13. 15 _____

14. 88 _____

15. 104 _____

16. 284 _____

17. 510 _____

18. 185 _____

Published by Frank Schaffer Publications. Copyright Protected.

0-7682-3112-4 *Place Value*

Representation

One Hundred More or Less

Write the number that is 100 more than the number given.

1. 365 _____

2. 38 _____

3. 198 _____

4. 793 _____

5. 226 _____

6. 430 _____

7. 648 _____

8. 744 _____

9. 50 _____

10. 576 _____

Write the number that is 100 less than the number given.

11. 159 _____

12. 200 _____

13. 929 _____

14. 610 _____

15. 111 _____

16. 315 _____

17. 672 _____

18. 138 _____

Published by Frank Schaffer Publications. Copyright Protected.

0-7682-3112-4 *Place Value*

How Many in All?

Solve each problem. Write each answer in expanded form.
Then write the answer in standard form.

1. Dylan's father gave him 100 baseball
   cards to add to his collection. He
   had 40 cards. Scott gave him
   5 more cards. How many cards
   does Dylan have now?

   _____

   _____

2. Chai has 100 beads in one box.
   She has another box with 70 beads.
   Chai finds 4 more beads on the floor.
   How many beads does Chai have in all?

   _____

   _____

3. Mrs. Jay has one bag of 200 chocolate chips. She has
   another bag with 80 chips. How many chocolate chips
   does Mrs. Jay have?

   _____

   _____

Published by Frank Schaffer Publications. Copyright Protected.

0-7682-3112-4 *Place Value*

Name_____ Date _____

Not All Nations Are Big

Use the information in each statement to fill in the blanks.

Do You Know?
Social
Studies

1. The nation of Andorra has an area of 174 square miles.

    174 means _____ hundreds 7 _____ 4 ones.

2. The nation of Bahrain has an area of 2__0 square miles.
    This number means _____ hundreds 4 tens _____ ones.

3. The nation of Barbados has an area of _____ square
    miles, which means 1 hundred 6 tens 5 ones.

4. The nation of Comoros has an area of _____ 0 square
    miles, which means 8 hundreds 4 tens _____ ones.

5. The nation of Maldives has an area of ____1____ square
    miles. This number means 1 hundred _____ tens 5 ones.

More Facts
The smallest nations of Monaco and Vatican City each
have an area less than 1 square mile.

Published by Frank Schaffer Publications. Copyright Protected.

0-7682-3112-4 *Place Value*

Communication

Name_____ Date _____

Guide the Bears

Help the bears find their cave. Match the number on each
bear to the correct expanded form on the cave. Draw a line
to show the match. Two bears do not have a cave.

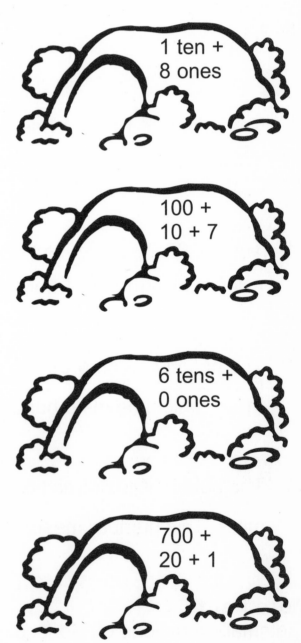

1 ten +
8 ones

100 +
10 + 7

6 tens +
0 ones

700 +
20 + 1

Published by Frank Schaffer Publications. Copyright Protected.

0-7682-3112-4 *Place Value*

Name_____ Date _____

Dimes and Pennies

A dime has the same value as a ten. A penny has the same value as a one. Complete the table for each amount.

1.

56

_____ tens _____ ones

_____ dimes _____ pennies

_____¢

2.

28

_____ tens _____ ones

_____ dimes _____ pennies

_____¢

3.

9

_____ tens _____ ones

_____ dimes _____ pennies

_____¢

4.

77

_____ tens _____ ones

_____ dimes _____ pennies

_____¢

5.

15

_____ ten _____ ones

_____ dime _____ pennies

_____¢

6.

40

_____ tens _____ ones

_____ dimes _____ pennies

_____¢

Published by Frank Schaffer Publications. Copyright Protected.

0-7682-3112-4 *Place Value*

Money in the Bank

How much money is in each bank?

1.

_____

2.

_____

3.

_____

4.

_____

Published by Frank Schaffer Publications. Copyright Protected.

0-7682-3112-4 *Place Value*

Connections

Which Purse Has the Most?

Draw a line to match each set of coins to the purse with the matching amount shown.

Color the purse with the most money green.
Color the purse with one dime red.
Color the purse with the most number of pennies blue.

1.  **2.**  **3.**  **4.**

5.  **6.**  **7.**

 7¢

24¢

 14¢

42¢

 43¢

23¢

 32¢

Published by Frank Schaffer Publications. Copyright Protected.

0-7682-3112-4 *Place Value*

Connections

Name_____ Date _____

Model the Money

Complete the table for each amount.

	Amount	Model of Money	Expanded Form
1.	71¢		70¢ + 1¢
2.	16¢		
3.	55¢		
4.	24¢		
5.	32¢		

Published by Frank Schaffer Publications. Copyright Protected.

0-7682-3112-4 *Place Value*

Money for Shopping

Look at the price tag on each item. Write the number of
dimes and the number of pennies needed to buy the item.

1.

_____dimes _____ pennies

2.

_____dimes _____ pennies

3.

_____dimes _____ pennies

4.

_____dimes _____ pennies

5.

_____dimes _____ pennies

6.

_____dimes _____ pennies

Published by Frank Schaffer Publications. Copyright Protected.

0-7682-3112-4 *Place Value*

Counting Tally Marks

Skip count by 5 to find the total number of tally marks.

1.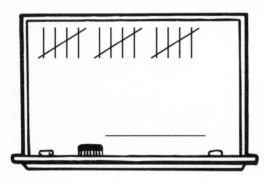

2.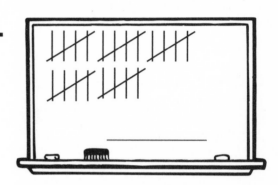

3.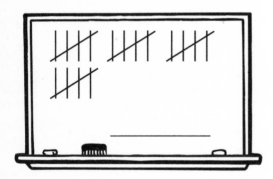

4.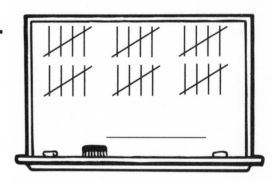

Count to find the total number of tally marks.

5.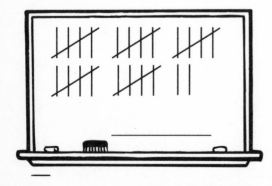

6.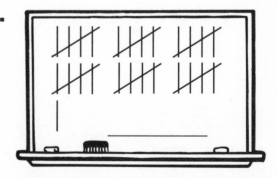

Published by Frank Schaffer Publications. Copyright Protected.

0-7682-3112-4 *Place Value*

Connections

Making Tally Marks

Name_____ Date _____

Make tally marks in groups of five for each number.
Use single tally marks as needed.

1. 18

2. 22

3. 5

4. 14

5. 31

6. 7

7. 10

8. 4

Count all the tally marks you made
in questions 1 - 8. Write the total
in the sign the boys are holding.

Published by Frank Schaffer Publications. Copyright Protected.

0-7682-3112-4 *Place Value*

Representation

Name _____ Date _____

Same Number, Different Name

Circle sets of ten. Count each set of birds. Write the
number two different ways.

1.

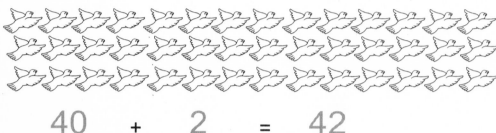

___40___ + ___2___ = ___42___

___10___ + ___30___ + ___2___ = ___42___

2.

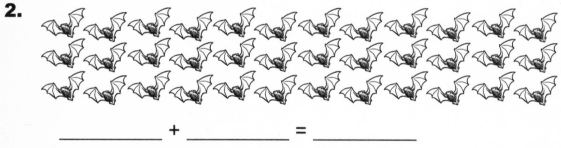

_____ + _____ = _____

_____ + _____ + _____ = _____

3.

_____ + _____ = _____

_____ + _____ + _____ = _____

Published by Frank Schaffer Publications. Copyright Protected.

0-7682-3112-4 *Place Value*

Representation

Name_____ Date _____

Make Sets of Ten

Circle sets of ten. Write how many of each.

1.

_____ tens + _____

_____ raindrops

2.

_____ tens + _____

_____ flowers

3.

_____ tens + _____

_____ faces

Published by Frank Schaffer Publications. Copyright Protected.

0-7682-3112-4 *Place Value*

Communication

Tens and Ones Chart

Complete the chart for each number.

1. 78

tens	ones

2. 12

tens	ones

3. 43

tens	ones

4. 58

tens	ones

5. 30

tens	ones

6. 64

tens	ones

7. 8

tens	ones

8. 99

tens	ones

Published by Frank Schaffer Publications. Copyright Protected.

0-7682-3112-4 *Place Value*

More Tens and Ones Charts

Name_____ Date _____

Write the number given in each chart in standard form and word form.

1.

tens	ones
2	7

_____

_____

2.

tens	ones
4	1

_____

_____

3.

tens	ones
5	8

_____

_____

4.

tens	ones
9	2

_____

_____

5.

tens	ones
3	6

_____

_____

6.

tens	ones
8	0

_____

_____

Published by Frank Schaffer Publications. Copyright Protected.

0-7682-3112-4 *Place Value*

Representation

Name_____ Date _____

Place Value Blocks

Name the number modeled in the chart.

1.

tens	ones

_____

2.

tens	ones

_____

3.

tens	ones

_____

4.

tens	ones

_____

5.

tens	ones

_____

6.

tens	ones

_____

7.

tens	ones

_____

8.

tens	ones

_____

Published by Frank Schaffer Publications. Copyright Protected.

0-7682-3112-4 *Place Value*

Renaming Ones

Count the number of ones blocks. When there are 10 or more ones blocks, rename 10 ones to 1 ten. Write the number in standard form.

1.

tens	ones

____4____ tens + ____12____ ones

____5____ tens + ____2____ ones

____52____

2.

tens	ones

_____ ten + _____ ones

_____ tens + _____ ones

_____

3.

tens	ones

_____ tens + _____ ones

_____ tens + _____ ones

_____

4.

tens	ones

_____ tens + _____ ones

_____ tens + _____ ones

_____

Published by Frank Schaffer Publications. Copyright Protected.

0-7682-3112-4 *Place Value*

Reasoning and Proof

Rename in Standard Form

Rewrite each number so that there are less than
10 ones. Then write the number in standard form.

1. 5 tens + 16 ones

_____ tens + _____ ones

_____

2. 1 ten + 19 ones

_____ tens + _____ ones

_____

3. 2 tens + 11 ones

_____ tens + _____ ones

_____

4. 3 tens + 15 ones

_____ tens + _____ ones

_____

5. 8 tens + 14 ones

_____ tens + _____ ones

_____

6. 4 tens + 20 ones

_____ tens + _____ ones

_____

7. 6 tens + 10 ones

_____ tens + _____ ones

_____

8. 2 tens + 17 ones

_____ tens + _____ ones

_____

Published by Frank Schaffer Publications. Copyright Protected.

0-7682-3112-4 *Place Value*

Write in Several Ways

Write each number in the ways described.

1. 122

Write in expanded form using 12 ones.

100 + 10 + 12

Write in expanded form using 20.

_____

Write in expanded form using 12 tens.

_____

2. 815

Write in expanded form using 800.

_____

Write in expanded form using 15 ones.

_____

Write in word form using fifteen.

_____

Published by Frank Schaffer Publications. Copyright Protected.

0-7682-3112-4 *Place Value*

Model the Missing Blocks

Problem Solving

Draw place value blocks so that each model matches the number given.

1. 77

tens	ones

2. 61

tens	ones

3. 58

tens	ones

4. 84

tens	ones

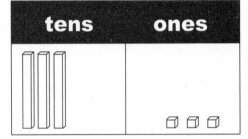

5. 25

tens	ones

6. 16

tens	ones

Published by Frank Schaffer Publications. Copyright Protected.

0-7682-3112-4 *Place Value*

Name_____ Date _____

Hundreds, Tens, and Ones Chart

Complete the chart for each number.

1. 168

hundreds	tens	ones

2. 142

hundreds	tens	ones

3. 379

hundreds	tens	ones

4. 198

hundreds	tens	ones

5. 320

hundreds	tens	ones

6. 514

hundreds	tens	ones

7. 805

hundreds	tens	ones

8. 700

hundreds	tens	ones

Published by Frank Schaffer Publications. Copyright Protected.

0-7682-3112-4 *Place Value*

Name_____ Date _____

Hundreds in Charts

Write the number given in each chart in expanded form and standard form.

1.

hundreds	tens	ones
1	8	1

_____

_____

2.

hundreds	tens	ones
2	2	9

_____

_____

3.

hundreds	tens	ones
5	7	2

_____

_____

4.

hundreds	tens	ones
8	0	4

_____

_____

5.

hundreds	tens	ones
1	4	0

_____

_____

6.

hundreds	tens	ones
7	3	6

_____

_____

Published by Frank Schaffer Publications. Copyright Protected.

0-7682-3112-4 *Place Value*

More Place Value Blocks

Connections

Name the number modeled in each chart.

1.

hundreds	tens	ones

_____

2.

hundreds	tens	ones

_____

3.

hundreds	tens	ones

_____

4.

hundreds	tens	ones

_____

Published by Frank Schaffer Publications. Copyright Protected.

0-7682-3112-4 *Place Value*

Renaming Tens

Count the number of tens blocks in each chart. When there are 10 or more tens blocks, rename 10 tens to 1 hundred. Write the number in standard form.

1.

hundreds	tens	ones

_____ hundreds + _____ tens + _____ ones

_____ hundreds + _____ ten + _____ ones

_____

2.

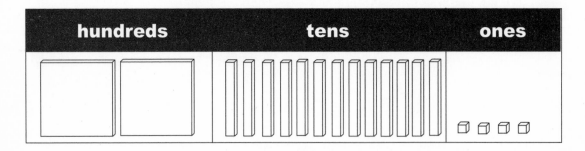

hundreds	tens	ones

_____ hundreds + _____ tens + _____ ones

_____ hundreds + _____ tens + _____ ones

_____

Published by Frank Schaffer Publications. Copyright Protected.

0-7682-3112-4 *Place Value*

Reasoning and Proof

Rename in Standard Form

Rewrite each number so that there are less than
10 tens. Then write the number in standard form.

1. 3 hundreds + 15 tens + 6 ones

_____ hundreds + _____ tens + _____ ones

_____

2. 9 hundreds + 11 tens + 2 ones

_____ hundreds + _____ ten + _____ ones

_____

3. 5 hundreds + 15 tens + 5 ones

_____ hundreds + _____ tens + _____ ones

_____

4. 2 hundreds + 20 tens + 7 ones

_____ hundreds + _____ tens + _____ ones

_____

Published by Frank Schaffer Publications. Copyright Protected.

0-7682-3112-4 *Place Value*

Model the Missing Blocks

Draw place value blocks so that each model matches the number.

1. 167

hundreds	tens	ones

2. 244

hundreds	tens	ones

3. 259

hundreds	tens	ones

4. 123

hundreds	tens	ones

Published by Frank Schaffer Publications. Copyright Protected.

0-7682-3112-4 *Place Value*

Representation

Creating Models

Use place value blocks to create a model of each number.

1. 4

2. 14

3. 214

4. 162

5. 62

6. 2

Published by Frank Schaffer Publications. Copyright Protected.

0-7682-3112-4 *Place Value*

Reasoning and Proof

Rename Ones, Then Tens

Rewrite each number so that there are less than
10 ones, and then less than 10 tens. Then write the
number in standard form.

1. 2 hundreds + 12 tens + 14 ones

_____ hundreds + _____ tens + _____ ones

_____

2. 6 hundreds + 10 tens + 16 ones

_____ hundreds + _____ ten + _____ ones

_____

3. 3 hundreds + 17 tens + 18 ones

_____ hundreds + _____ tens + _____ ones

_____

4. 1 hundreds + 10 tens + 20 ones

_____ hundreds + _____ tens + _____ ones

_____

Published by Frank Schaffer Publications. Copyright Protected.

0-7682-3112-4 *Place Value*

Name_____ Date _____

Skip Count by Ten

Circle sets of ten until all objects are counted.
Skip count by ten to find the total number of objects.

1. ✳✳✳✳✳✳✳✳✳✳✳✳✳✳✳✳✳✳✳✳✳✳✳✳✳✳✳✳✳✳
✳✳✳✳✳✳✳✳✳✳✳✳✳✳✳✳✳✳✳✳✳✳✳✳✳✳✳✳✳✳
✳✳✳✳✳✳✳✳✳✳✳✳✳✳✳✳✳✳✳✳✳✳✳✳✳✳✳✳✳✳

_____

2. ✓✓✓✓✓✓✓✓✓✓✓✓✓✓✓✓✓✓✓✓✓✓✓✓✓✓✓✓
✓✓✓✓✓✓✓✓✓✓✓✓✓✓✓✓✓✓✓✓✓✓✓✓✓✓✓✓
✓✓✓✓✓✓✓✓✓✓✓✓✓✓✓✓✓✓✓✓✓✓

_____

3. ✏✏✏✏✏✏✏✏✏✏✏✏✏✏✏✏✏✏✏✏✏✏✏✏✏✏✏✏✏
✏✏✏✏✏✏✏✏✏✏✏✏✏✏✏✏✏✏✏✏✏✏✏✏✏✏✏✏✏
✏✏✏✏✏✏✏✏✏✏✏✏✏✏✏✏✏✏✏✏

_____

4. ❀❀❀❀❀❀❀❀❀❀❀❀❀❀❀❀❀❀❀❀❀❀❀❀❀❀❀❀❀❀
❀❀❀❀❀❀❀❀❀❀❀❀❀❀❀❀❀❀❀❀❀❀❀❀❀❀❀❀❀❀
❀❀❀❀❀❀❀❀❀❀❀❀❀❀❀❀❀❀❀❀❀❀❀❀❀❀❀❀❀❀
❀❀❀❀❀❀❀❀❀❀❀❀❀❀❀❀❀❀❀❀❀❀❀❀❀

_____

Published by Frank Schaffer Publications. Copyright Protected.

0-7682-3112-4 *Place Value*

Representation

Name______________________________ Date ___________________

What Does 100 Look Like?

Circle sets of ten. Count the sets. How many objects in all?

1. ✽✽✽✽✽✽✽✽✽✽✽✽✽✽✽✽✽✽✽✽✽✽✽✽✽✽✽✽✽✽
✽✽✽✽✽✽✽✽✽✽✽✽✽✽✽✽✽✽✽✽✽✽✽✽✽✽✽✽✽✽
✽✽✽✽✽✽✽✽✽✽✽✽✽✽✽✽✽✽✽✽✽✽✽✽✽✽✽✽✽✽
✽✽✽✽✽✽✽✽✽✽

____

2. ✘✘✘✘✘✘✘✘✘✘✘✘✘✘✘✘✘✘✘✘✘✘✘✘✘
✘✘✘✘✘✘✘✘✘✘✘✘✘✘✘✘✘✘✘✘✘✘✘✘✘
✘✘✘✘✘✘✘✘✘✘✘✘✘✘✘✘✘✘✘✘✘✘✘✘✘
✘✘✘✘✘✘✘✘✘✘✘✘✘✘✘✘✘✘✘✘✘✘✘✘✘

____

3. ✍ ✍ ✍ ✍ ✍ ✍ ✍ ✍ ✍ ✍ ✍ ✍ ✍ ✍ ✍ ✍ ✍ ✍
✍ ✍ ✍ ✍ ✍ ✍ ✍ ✍ ✍ ✍ ✍ ✍ ✍ ✍ ✍ ✍ ✍ ✍
✍ ✍ ✍ ✍ ✍ ✍ ✍ ✍ ✍ ✍ ✍ ✍ ✍ ✍ ✍ ✍ ✍ ✍
✍ ✍ ✍ ✍ ✍ ✍ ✍ ✍ ✍ ✍ ✍ ✍ ✍ ✍ ✍ ✍ ✍ ✍
✍ ✍ ✍ ✍ ✍ ✍ ✍ ✍ ✍ ✍ ✍ ✍ ✍ ✍ ✍ ✍ ✍ ✍
✍ ✍ ✍ ✍ ✍ ✍ ✍ ✍ ✍ ✍

____

Published by Frank Schaffer Publications. Copyright Protected.

0-7682-3112-4 *Place Value*

Use Ten to Estimate

Circle one set of ten. Estimate how many objects in all.

1.

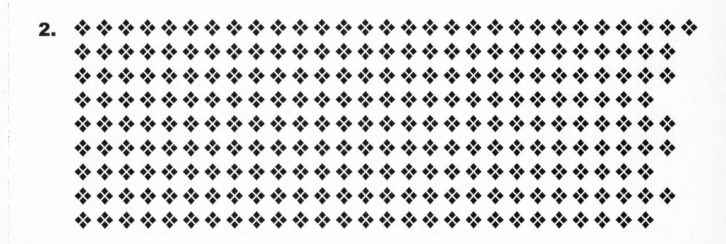

_____

2.

_____

Published by Frank Schaffer Publications. Copyright Protected.

0-7682-3112-4 *Place Value*

Reasoning and Proof

Name_____ Date _____

Estimate if Greater Than 100

Circle one set of ten. Estimate if there are more or less than 100 objects. Circle the correct answer.

1.

more than 100   less than 100

2.

more than 100   less than 100

3.

more than 100   less than 100

4.

more than 100   less than 100

Published by Frank Schaffer Publications. Copyright Protected.

0-7682-3112-4 *Place Value*

Number Lines

Name the numbers that are missing on each number line.

1.

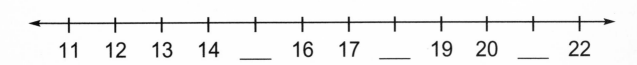

11 12 13 14 ___ 16 17 ___ 19 20 ___ 22

2.

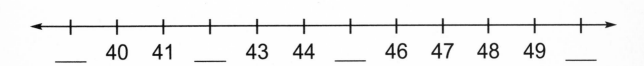

___ 40 41 ___ 43 44 ___ 46 47 48 49 ___

3.

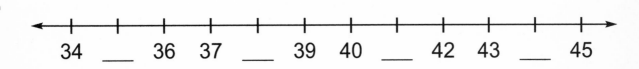

34 ___ 36 37 ___ 39 40 ___ 42 43 ___ 45

4.

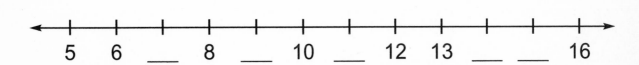

60 ___ 62 ___ 64 65 66 ___ 68 69 ___ ___

5.

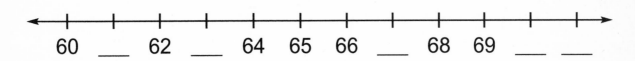

5 6 ___ 8 ___ 10 ___ 12 13 ___ ___ 16

Published by Frank Schaffer Publications. Copyright Protected.

0-7682-3112-4 *Place Value*

Representation

Name_____ Date _____

Put the Books in Order

Look at the numbers on the books below. Write the numbers in the blanks along the bottom from least to greatest.

_____   _____   _____   _____

_____   _____   _____   _____

_____   _____   _____   _____

Published by Frank Schaffer Publications. Copyright Protected.   0-7682-3112-4 *Place Value*

Communication

Name_____ Date _____

What Number is Next?

Name the number that comes after the one on the first elephant.

1.
86

2.
18

3.
22

4.
53

5.
71

6.
84

7.
90

8.
45

75

Published by Frank Schaffer Publications. Copyright Protected.

0-7682-3112-4 *Place Value*

Problem Solving

Name_____ Date _____

The Seat in Between

Write the missing numbers in place on each seat.

Row J

101 ___ ___ 104

Row D

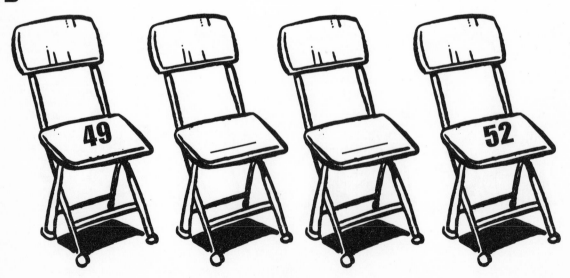

49 ___ ___ 52

Published by Frank Schaffer Publications. Copyright Protected.

0-7682-3112-4 *Place Value*

Name_____ Date _____

Room Numbers

Name the room number that comes before and after each room number shown.

1.

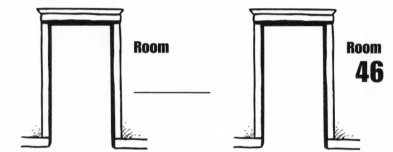

Room
_____

Room
46

Room
_____

2.

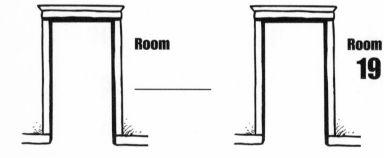

Room
_____

Room
19

Room
_____

3.

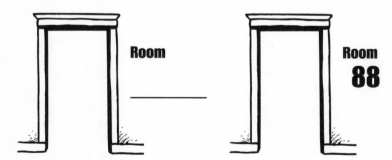

Room
_____

Room
88

Room
_____

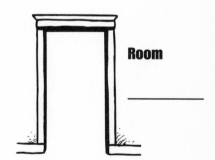

Published by Frank Schaffer Publications. Copyright Protected.

0-7682-3112-4 *Place Value*

Count From Top to Bottom

Use a different colored crayon to trace a path of numbers in order from each top cell to one of the bottom cells.

6	14	27	42	76	92
15	7	43	28	93	77
8	16	29	44	94	78
9	30	17	45	79	95
31	10	18	80	46	96
32	19	11	81	97	47
20	33	82	12	48	98
21	83	34	49	13	99
84	22	35	14	50	100
23	85	15	36	101	51
24	16	86	102	37	52
17	25	103	87	53	38

Published by Frank Schaffer Publications. Copyright Protected.

0-7682-3112-4 *Place Value*

Name_____ Date _____

From Start to Finish

Fill in the missing numbers from start to finish.

Published by Frank Schaffer Publications. Copyright Protected.

0-7682-3112-4 *Place Value*

Name_____ Date _____

The Horse in the Middle

Write the number that comes between the numbers given on the horses in each row.

1.

2.

3.

4.

Published by Frank Schaffer Publications. Copyright Protected.

0-7682-3112-4 *Place Value*

Up and Away

Place the numbers of each pair in the balloons. Put the greater number in the balloon that is higher up.

1. 45, 36

2. 60, 90

3. 13, 31

4. 55, 53

5. 86, 28

6. 99, 101

Published by Frank Schaffer Publications. Copyright Protected.

0-7682-3112-4 *Place Value*

Name_____ Date _____

Duck Pond

Mr. Howard is working the Duck Pond game. In the morning, the player who selects the duck with the lesser number wins. Circle the duck that wins.

1.

2.

3.

4.

In the afternoon, the player who selects the duck with the greater number wins. Circle the duck that wins.

5.

6.

7.

8.

Published by Frank Schaffer Publications. Copyright Protected.

0-7682-3112-4 *Place Value*

Communication

Pick a Monster

Use the number on the backs of the monsters to complete each statement.

1.

_____ > _____

2.

_____ < _____

3.

_____ < _____

4.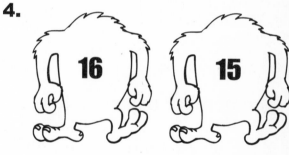

_____ > _____

5.

_____ > _____

6.

_____ > _____

Published by Frank Schaffer Publications. Copyright Protected.

0-7682-3112-4 *Place Value*

Lasso Numbers

Cowboy Bob needs to lasso the number described in each question. Circle the number that he should lasso.

1. The number that is 100 greater than 355.

255   356   365   455

2. The number that is 1 less than 125.

126   124   26   24

3. The number that is 10 less than 416.

315   316   406   426

4. The number that is 20 greater than 240.

40   220   242   260

5. The number that is 100 less than 130.

30   120   129   230

Published by Frank Schaffer Publications. Copyright Protected.

0-7682-3112-4 *Place Value*

Post Test

1. Which number has a 9 in the hundreds place?

   a. 9   **b.** 92   **c.** 99   **d.** 926   _____

2. Natalie is thinking of a number greater than 100 and less than 120. The number has a 1 in the tens place and a 4 in the ones place. What number is Natalie thinking of?   _____

3. What is the value of the underlined digit?

   93<u>4</u>   _____

4. Write the number 502 in expanded form.

   _____

5. 3 hundreds, 9 tens, and 2 ones = _____ + _____ + 2

6. Write 305 in word form.

   _____

7. Write the number that is 100 greater than 415.

Published by Frank Schaffer Publications. Copyright Protected.

0-7682-3112-4 *Place Value*

Post Test (cont.)

8. Gretchen has 82 cents. Gretchen has _____ dimes and _____ pennies.

9. Count the number of tally marks.

_____

10. What number is modeled? _____

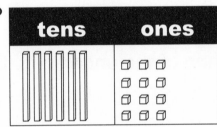

11. Rewrite 2 hundreds, 14 tens, and 2 ones in expanded form so there are less than 10 tens.

_____

12. Write the numbers below in order from least to greatest.

43, 34, 55, 48, 29

____ ____ ____ ____ ____

Published by Frank Schaffer Publications. Copyright Protected.

0-7682-3112-4 *Place Value*

Answer Key

Pretest 7-8
1. c.
2. 15
3. 500
4. 800 + 30 + 2
5. 2
6. ninety two
7. 819
8. 5, 3
9. 15
10. 3 tens, 4 ones
11. 2 blocks in hundreds column, 3 blocks in tens column, 5 blocks in ones column
12. 33

Happy Birthday to Ones 9

Plenty of Fruit 10
1. 7
2. 5
3. 8
4. 4
5. 6

Groups of 10 and More 11
1. 10 + 6 = 16
2. 10 + 3 = 13
3. 10 + 8 = 18
4. 10 + 5 = 15
5. 10 + 7 = 17

Match the Carrots 12

House Numbers .13
1. do not color
2. do not color
3. color
4. color
5. do not color
6. color

Pictures and Words 14
1. 5, five
2. 12, twelve
3. 10, ten
4. 7, seven

What's in the Picture? 15
1. 6
2. 8
3. 8
4. 6
5. less
6. pancakes

What is Tony's Number? 16
16

Ones, Tens, Hundreds 17
1. tens
2. hundreds
3. ones
4. tens
5. hundreds
6. tens
7. ones
8. ones
9. 5
10. 7
11. 1
12. 2
13. 0
14. 5

Name That Value 18
1. hundreds, 200
2. ones, 4
3. tens, 0
4. ones, 1
5. tens, 50
6. tens, 10
7. hundreds, 700
8. ones, 9

Published by Frank Schaffer Publications. Copyright Protected.

0-7682-3112-4 *Place Value*

Answer Key

Name That Number 19

1.	7	**2.**	2
3.	1	**4.**	9
5.	1	**6.**	6
7.	2	**8.**	4
9.	9	**10.**	6
11.	5	**12.**	9
13.	0	**14.**	4
15.	8	**16.**	0

How Many? 20

1.	8	**2.**	5
3.	4	**4.**	2
5.	9	**6.**	6
7.	5	**8.**	0
9.	2	**10.**	7
11.	1	**12.**	4
13.	3	**14.**	6
15.	1	**16.**	3

Value of a Digit 21

1.	20	**2.**	800
3.	1	**4.**	200
5.	70	**6.**	4

Rewrite From Expanded Form 22

1.	128	**2.**	362
3.	594	**4.**	190
5.	42	**6.**	706
7.	815	**8.**	222
9.	392	**10.**	470

Don't Look Down 23

1.	400 + 10 + 5	**2.**	300 + 80
3.	300 + 10 + 8	**4.**	200 + 50 +9
5.	300 + 10		

Numbers in Standard Form 24

1.	27	**2.**	840
3.	111	**4.**	80
5.	32	**6.**	659
7.	31	**8.**	99
9.	106		

What Color is the Wibble? 25

Color 800, 30, and 2 Wibbles green.
Color 100, 50, and 9 Wibbles red.
Color 600, 70, and 3 Wibbles blue.

Bunches of Balloons .26

Orders that the numbers are placed in the balloons may vary. Numbers with 5 in the ones place:

285 415 305 825 145 335 45

Numbers with 5 in the tens place:

152 550 652

What Number Am I? .27

1.	44	**2.**	21
3.	56	**4.**	98
5.	36	**6.**	76

Who is Reading What Book? 28

1. Sally read the book with 88 pages
2. Marc read the book with 150 pages.
3. Joel read the book with 111 pages.
4. Myra read the book with 27 pages.

Color to Reveal 29

Published by Frank Schaffer Publications. Copyright Protected.

0-7682-3112-4 *Place Value*

Answer Key

Banners of Numbers 30
1. 48   2. 61
3. 15   4. 94
5. 88

Who Lives Longer? .31
1. Black Bear
2. Horse
3. Tortoise
4. Human
5. Bald Eagle

What is Missing? 32
1. 543   2. 8
3. 80   4. 20
5. eleven   6. 40
7. fifteen   8. 757

Find Each Path 33

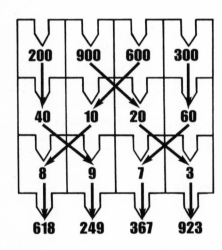

Place Value Riddles .34
1. 79
   I have 9 tens and 7 ones. What number am I?;
   97
2. 83
   I have an odd number of tens. What number
   am I?; 54
3. 12
   I have one more ten than ones. What number
   am I?; 32
4. 802
   I have 8 hundreds, 2 tens, and 0 ones. What
   number am I?; 820

Building Ice Cream Cones 35

200 / 80 / 1 — 281
700 / 40 / 9 — 749
300 / 50 / 2 — 352
900 / 70 / 8 — 978

Expanding a Number 36
1. 70 + 8
   7 tens 8 ones
2. 20 + 5
   2 tens 5 ones
3. 10 + 4
   1 ten 4 ones
4. 40 + 1
   4 tens 1 one
5. 90 + 2
   9 tens 2 ones
6. 50 + 0
   5 tens 0 ones

Take the Elevator 37
1. b
2. a
3. c
4. d

Picking from the Apple Tree 38
1. 100 + 20 + 3
2. 50 + 2
3. 800 + 10 + 3
4. 700 + 6
5. 832
6. 240
7. 106
8. 551

Write the Number 39
1. 873   2. 324
3. 600   4. 76
5. 641   6. 555

Published by Frank Schaffer Publications. Copyright Protected.

0-7682-3112-4 *Place Value*

Answer Key

Ten More or Ten Less 40
1. 28   2. 95   3. 23
4. 77   5. 52   6. 32
7. 61   8. 49   9. 80
10. 122   11. 153   12. 130
13. 5   14. 78   15. 94
16. 274   17. 500   18. 175

One Hundred More or Less 41
1. 465   2. 138
3. 298   4. 893
5. 326   6. 530
7. 748   8. 844
9. 150   10. 676
11. 59   12. 100
13. 829   14. 510
15. 11   16. 215
17. 572   18. 38

How Many in All? .42
1. 100 + 40 + 5, 145
2. 100 + 70 + 4, 174
3. 200 + 80, 280

Not All Nations Are Big 43
1. 1; tens
2. 4; 2; 0
3. 165
4. 84; 0
5. 1; 5; 1

Guide the Bears 44

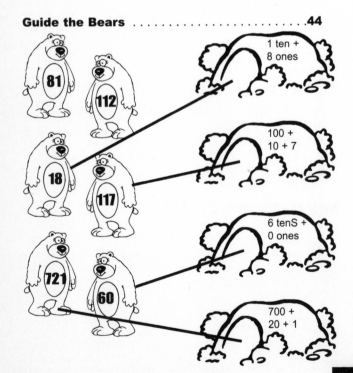

Dimes and Pennies 45
1. 5 tens 6 ones   2. 2 tens 8 ones
   5 dimes 6 pennies   2 dimes 8 pennies
   56¢   28¢
3. 0 tens 9 ones   4. 7 tens 7 ones
   0 dimes 9 pennies   7 dimes 7 pennies
   9¢   77¢
5. 1 ten 5 ones   6. 4 tens 0 ones
   1 dime 5 pennies   4 dimes 0 pennies
   15¢   40¢

Money in the Bank 46
1. 62¢   2. 25¢
3. 35¢   4. 81¢

Which Purse Has the Most? 47

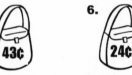

7. Color 43¢ purse green.
   Color 14¢ purse red.
   Color 7¢ purse blue.

Model the Money .48
1. 70¢ + 1¢
2. 10¢ + 6¢
3. 50¢ + 5¢
4. 20¢ + 4¢
5. 30¢ + 2¢

Money for Shopping 49
1. 7 dimes 9 pennies   2. 2 dimes 5 pennies
3. 4 dimes 8 pennies   4. 9 dimes 2 pennies
5. 5 dimes 5 pennies   6. 7 dimes 2 pennies

Published by Frank Schaffer Publications. Copyright Protected.

0-7682-3112-4 *Place Value*

Answer Key

1. 15
2. 25
3. 20
4. 30
5. 27
6. 31

1. ՄՏՐ ՄՏՐ ՄՏՐ |||
2. ՄՏՐ ՄՏՐ ՄՏՐ ՄՏՐ ||
3. ՄՏՐ
4. ՄՏՐ ՄՏՐ ||||
5. ՄՏՐ ՄՏՐ ՄՏՐ ՄՏՐ ՄՏՐ ՄՏՐ |
6. ՄՏՐ ||
7. ՄՏՐ ՄՏՐ
8. ||||

111 tally marks total

Circled sets will vary. Ways for writing numbers will vary. Sample answers are given.
1. 40 + 2 = 42
    10 + 30 + 2 = 42
2. 30 + 6 = 36
    10 + 20 + 6 = 36
3. 20 + 0 = 20
    10 + 10 + 0 = 20

Circled sets will vary.
1. 2 tens + 8
    28 raindrops
2. 2 tens + 1
    21 flowers
3. 2 tens + 4
    24 faces

1. 7 tens 8 ones
2. 1 ten 2 ones
3. 4 tens 3 ones
4. 5 tens 8 ones
5. 3 tens 0 ones
6. 6 tens 4 ones
7. 0 tens 8 ones
8. 9 tens 9 ones

1. 27, twenty-seven
2. 41, forty-one
3. 58, fifty-eight
4. 92, ninety-two
5. 36, thirty-six
6. 80, eighty

1. 74
2. 56
3. 47
4. 48
5. 33
6. 20
7. 61
8. 19

1. 4 tens + 12 ones
    5 tens + 2 ones
    52
2. 1 ten + 14 ones
    2 tens + 4 ones
    24
3. 2 tens + 10 ones
    3 tens + 0 ones
    30
4. 6 tens + 13 ones
    7 tens + 3 ones
    73

1. 6 tens + 6 ones
    66
2. 2 tens + 9 ones
    29
3. 3 tens + 1 one
    31
4. 4 tens + 5 ones
    45
5. 9 tens + 4 ones
    94
6. 6 tens + 0 ones
    60
7. 7 tens + 0 ones
    70
8. 3 tens + 7 ones
    37

1. 100 + 10 + 12
    100 + 20 + 2
    120 + 2
2. 800 + 10 + 5 or 800 + 15
    800 + 15
    eight hundred fifteen

Complete models are shown.

Published by Frank Schaffer Publications. Copyright Protected.

0-7682-3112-4 *Place Value*

Answer Key

3. tens   ones

4. tens   ones

5. tens   ones

6. tens   ones

Hundreds, Tens, and Ones Chart 61
1. 1 hundred 6 tens 8 ones
2. 1 hundred 4 tens 2 ones
3. 3 hundreds 7 tens 9 ones
4. 1 hundred 9 tens 8 ones
5. 3 hundreds 2 tens 0 ones
6. 5 hundreds 1 ten 4 ones
7. 8 hundreds 0 tens 5 ones
8. 7 hundreds 0 tens 0 ones

Hundreds in Charts 62
1. 100 + 80 + 1
   181
2. 200 + 20 + 9
   229
3. 500 + 70 + 2
   572
4. 800 + 4
   804
5. 100 + 40
   140
6. 700 + 30 + 6
   736

More Place Value Blocks 63
1. 134
2. 222
3. 169
4. 210

Renaming Tens 64
1. 1 hundreds + 11 tens + 5 ones
   2 hundreds + 1 ten + 5 ones
   215
2. 2 hundreds + 13 tens + 4 ones
   3 hundreds + 3 tens + 4 ones
   334

Rename in Standard Form 65
1. 4 hundreds + 5 tens + 6 ones
   456
2. 10 hundreds + 1 ten + 2 ones
   1012
3. 6 hundreds + 5 tens + 5 ones
   655
4. 4 hundreds + 7 ones
   407

Model the Missing Blocks 66
Complete models are shown.

1. hundreds   tens   ones

2. hundreds   tens   ones

3. hundreds   tens   ones

4. hundreds   tens   ones

Creating Models 67

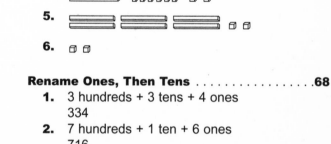

Rename Ones, Then Tens 68
1. 3 hundreds + 3 tens + 4 ones
   334
2. 7 hundreds + 1 ten + 6 ones
   716
3. 4 hundreds + 8 tens + 8 ones
   488
4. 2 hundreds + 2 tens + 0 ones
   220

Skip Count by Ten 69
1. 90
2. 80
3. 60
4. 110

What Does 100 Look Like? 70
1. 100
2. 100
3. 100

Published by Frank Schaffer Publications. Copyright Protected.

0-7682-3112-4 *Place Value*

Answer Key

Use Ten to Estimate 71
Answers will vary. Sample answers are given.
1. 240   2. 250

Estimate if Greater Than 100 72
1. less than 100   2. more than 100
3. more than 100   4. less than 100

Number Lines 73
1.
   11 12 13 14 <u>15</u> 16 17 <u>18</u> 19 20 <u>21</u> 22
2.
   <u>39</u> 40 41 <u>42</u> 43 44 <u>45</u> 46 47 48 49 <u>50</u>
3.
   34 <u>35</u> 36 37 38 39 40 <u>41</u> 42 43 <u>44</u> 45
4.
   60 <u>61</u> 62 <u>63</u> 64 65 66 <u>67</u> 68 69 <u>70</u> <u>71</u>
5.
   5 6 <u>7</u> 8 <u>9</u> 10 <u>11</u> 12 13 <u>14</u> <u>15</u> 16

Put the Books in Order 74
25 26 27 28
29 30 31 32
33 34 35 36

What Number is Next? 75
1. 87   2. 19
3. 23   4. 54
5. 72   6. 85
7. 91   8. 46

The Seat in Between 76
Row J: 102, 103
Row D: 50, 51

Room Numbers 77
1. Room 45, Room 47
2. Room 18, Room 20
3. Room 87, Room 89

Count From Top to Bottom 78

From Start to Finish 79

The Horse in the Middle 80
1. 40   2. 17
3. 51   4. 99

Up and Away 81
1. 45 36
2. 90 60
3. 31 13
4. 55 53
5. 86 28
6. 101 99

93

Published by Frank Schaffer Publications. Copyright Protected.

0-7682-3112-4 *Place Value*

Answer Key

Duck Pond 82

1.	47	**2.**	14
3.	37	**4.**	41
5.	79	**6.**	72
7.	90	**8.**	60

Pick a Monster 83

1.	89 > 64	**2.**	26 < 48
3.	56 < 76	**4.**	16 > 15
5.	110 > 100	**6.**	47 > 41

Lasso Numbers 84

1.	455	**2.**	124
3.	406	**4.**	260
5.	30		

Post Test 85–86

1. d
2. 114
3. ones
4. 500 + 2
5. 300 + 90 + 2
6. three hundred five
7. 515
8. 8 dimes, 2 pennies
9. 32
10. 72
11. 300 + 40 + 2
12. 29, 34, 43, 48, 55

Published by Frank Schaffer Publications. Copyright Protected.

0-7682-3112-4 *Place Value*